THE
MYSTERIOUS
ROCKIES

TEXT AND PHOTOGRAPHS BY
GEORGE BRYBYCIN

GB PUBLISHING
CALGARY, ALBERTA

INTRODUCTION

This edition features the mysteries of light and colour in the Canadian Rockies – it may be small but it is large in concept and, therefore, unique. From startlingly beautiful sunrises and sunsets, to clear, starry nights, lightning, and the majestic Aurora Borealis, all are presented here in vivid hues.

The fiery ball of the sun sinks below the jagged skyline of the Rockies, we enter into the twilight zone. The total darkness of night may take up to two hours to descend, depending on latitude and time of year. Autumn and winter nights are long and allow camera buffs, who do not mind lurking animals, to get busy and create uniquely extraordinary and mysterious images.

Sunsets and sunrises in the Rockies are a true feast for the soul. No two are alike – every day has its own unique climactic conditions, affecting intensity and variety of colour. Sunsets tend to be more dramatic, due to natural conditions, man-made pollution, the heat of the day and other atmospheric factors. Sunrises, on the other hand, may be of less intense colour, but because of the cool of the night, and fewer human activities, the air is crisp and clear – affording conditions for the best photography.

As you leaf through this book, you will note that there are familiar patterns in each photo – red/pink at the top, darker below. Upon closer examination, you will begin to see differences in colour and texture – every image is very different and, therefore, unique and mysterious. You will also realize that this humble volume presents extraordinary light quality and ambience.

Photos like these are not taken during a single jaunt to the mountains. Indeed, one could comb the Rockies for days to find that the weather allows only a few opportunities to take even a few mediocre shots. Good luck, if you want to get the perfect photo of a reflection in Lake Minnewanka, for example – it is being exposed to open valley winds makes that quite impossible.

Time exposures at night, present other obstacles – usually noticeable only after several rolls of film and a lot of time have been wasted. Shooting the night sky requires the camera to be tilted upward – after just an hour, dew can settle on the lens, rendering the photo hazy and useless.

Wind can shake the camera, producing out of focus shots; clouds may pass over, obscuring the stars' paths – producing dashes, instead of lines. What can you do? As persnickety as Mother Nature can get, she also can be generous. The trick is keep trying. Persistence has its rewards. Eventually you will get that one truly great photo.

That is why only a few individuals are able to make a living at nature photography. To get that perfect shot, they must love both photography and adventure – that requires a certain kind of passion. In a sense, paying the bills is secondary to the more physical, spiritual and social benefits of the work. The author gets plenty of healthy exercise in the fresh air; does not have to put up with ringing telephones; answers to no grumpy boss. Even better, he experiences the unexpected thrill of happening upon a great shot. For him, this is the world's best line of work.

Above: Not many people want to risk sleeping on ice or rock just to witness a sunset, or greet a new day, next morning. Here, the author experiences a brand new morning from atop Wonder Peak (2852m), looking southwest, near the beautiful Marvel Lake. Mt. Assiniboine Provincial Park.

Left: Bow Lake, along the Icefields Parkway, is known for its fine scenery and many moods. The early morning light casts gold-bronze hues on the lake and enchants a lone fisherman. Even if he doesn't catch one fish, what a privilege it is just to be here in paradise. Banff National Park.

Above: Moraine Lake is always mysterious – especially in a gorgeous, bronze sunrise. The "Ten Peaks" stand high, guarding the lake, which is the jewel of the Rockies. Visit the lake at dawn, and witness the mystery of your life. Banff National Park.

Left: Deltaform Mtn (3424m) is number eight of the "Ten Peaks". Only a low morning light shows the real topography of the place. Shadows reveal all. Super Couloir crosses the mountain from lower right to the summit, and rises 1125m above the valley. This is a long, arduous climb – often under atrocious conditions. Rated F8.5 or IV.

Above: Witnessing the mystery of sunrise from Wonder Peak (2852m) as Mt. Assiniboine (3618m) glows in the centre. The blue sky is synonymous with autumn in the Rockies (most years). Mt. Assiniboine Provincial Park.

Left: Spring is around the corner, in mid-April, and the thick ice on the Sunwapta River melts fast. Another month or so, and the valley will be full of runoff water from the Columbia Icefield. "Emergency camping" is at the Beauty Creek Youth Hostel. Jasper National Park.

Coincidentally, this photo was taken at the same location as the one on page 8 – only looking west. The day was overcast and it was raining heavily when, suddenly, at sunset, the clouds started turning red. The author slammed on the brakes, waited a moment, and then snapped a few frames, using no filters. Beauty Creek, northwest of the Columbia Icefield. Jasper National Park.

Not everyone who passes Mt. Robson (3954m) has seen the Monarch. Its high elevation and prevailing moist air obscures its peak 50-60% of the time. Because of that moisture, Mt. Robson is surrounded by rainforest, where the flora and fauna is remarkably rich. A patient, persistent photographer will eventually get that clear, gorgeous sunset one day. Mt. Robson Provincial Park.

It does not look like it, but this is Mt. Rundle (2998m), as seen from the east, along Lake Minnewanka Road. Every mountain has at least four faces, and each is different. The beauty of mountain climbing is the opportunity to see the previously unseen faces of known mountains. What rich colours and forms this mountain presents at sunrise. Banff National Park.

Bow Lake, along the Icefields Parkway, is beautiful – here, it is dressed up by the mysterious, rising moon, right between Mt. Hector and Bow Peak. The moon is romantic – Beethoven wrote his "Moonlight Sonata" and poets have written poems, but the photographer can only capture the moment for others to enjoy. Banff National Park.

Above: Athabasca Falls has as many moods as there are days in the year. Every time one sees it, it looks different. Here, in July, the water level is quite high. Close to sunset, the low light and mist creates a rainbow as the west face of Mt. Kerkeslin glows. What more could one ask for? Jasper National Park.

Left: Speaking of mystery, here is the spectacular Takakkaw Falls, in blue. This is a night photo with a long time exposure. Again, the mystery of the night is endless, and always surprising. Try the next night, and you will get a very different result. No two nights are the same, as our mood and perceptions change as well. Yoho National Park.

Above. It is early December, and the Athabasca River, just east of Jasper, is in the final stage of freeze-up. This gorgeous sunrise scene is only warm in the sense of its colours. It was –20°C when this photo was taken. It will be another four months before the river shrugs off these icy shackles for the summer.

Left: The same idea as above. Here, the Athabasca River winds its way toward Jasper, and then north and east down to the Prairies. The sun's "warm" rays illuminate the summit of Pyramid Mountain (2763m) on a crisp December morning. Jasper National Park.

Above: The last rays of the setting sun gently brush the summits of Castle Mtn. (2766m), a well known and loved landmark, halfway between Banff and Lake Louise. It is readily accessible by a good hiking trail to Rockbound Lake, then one circles the lake above the north side and trudges to the summit. It's a long walk, but a rewarding one. Banff National Park.

Left: Cathedral Crags (3073m) is just northwest summit of Cathedral Mtn (3189m) Massif – as craggy as it gets. It's not easy to climb, but was first ascended as early as 1900, Cathedral Mtn in 1901. Somehow, this mountain gets a lot of strong, colourful sunsets. This is one of them. Yoho National Park.

Above: Yoho National Park is rather small (1313 sq. km) but is blessed with many outstanding natural wonders. One of these is Emerald Lake, and the flamboyant Mt. Burgess (2599m) Being west of the Continental Divide, the park enjoys a fairly mild climate, allowing rare species of trees – like the Cedar, or Maple – to grow.

Left: Lit by the strong August sun, Cascade Mtn (2998m) basks in the glorious reds of sunrise. Viewed from the east, the mountain is just north of Banff, and readily accessible by a major trail to the west side amphitheatre. From there, it is just an easy scramble. The summit presents comprehensive views in all directions. Banff National Park.

Above: The Northern Lights, or Aurora Borealis (Goddess of the Dawn). An electric storm occurring in the upper atmosphere, its movement depends on the intensity of the solar winds. They occur in both north and south polar regions (Aurora Australis). They can be seen year round, but long winter nights provide more opportunities to view this mysterious phenomenon – which has no relation to cold. Mostly a silvery-greenish colour, though occasionally red and yellow.

Left: More mysteries of the night. Spectacular by nature, Maligne Lake is even better when adorned by the rising silver-gold moon. The Lake nestles high up in the mountains southeast of Jasper – accessible by a good road, year round. At night, keep checking over your shoulder – Grizzly Bears or Moose are never far away. The Lake is 22 km long – ideal for fabulous canoe trips. Jasper National Park.

Above: Pyramid Lake and Mountain (2763m) are located just north of Jasper. This is lake country – west of here can be seen dozens of lakes, of various sizes. They are accessible by a fine network of trails, where Moose, Elk, Deer and Bear can be seen. Jasper National Park.

Left: The awesome, fascinating Mt. Stephen (3199m) stands tall above the Kicking Horse River, and is one of the many major sights of Yoho National Park. For peaks baggers, this is a very big prize. A long day's climb, the elevation gain is nearly two kilometers, and the top section is not easy.

The morning mist lingers above cool Bow Lake as jagged Crowfoot Mountain (3050m) basks in the morning sun. The mountain consists of three rugged peaks of almost equal elevation, the southernmost being the highest. It was conquered in 1950. Banff National Park.

Bow Summit (2069m) is the highest point on the Icefields Parkway, between Lake Louise and Jasper. The area presents high alpine tundra and meadows, with related flora and fauna. It is a permanent home to Grizzly Bear. Moose frequent the heights to escape nasty summer bugs. Banff National Park.

Above and left: The mountain synonymous with Banff – Mt. Rundle (2998m) stands tall just southeast of Banff townsite. Named after missionary, Robert Rundle, who visited the area in 1847. Sulphur hot springs were then discovered, and to protect them, a small National Park – the first in Canada – was established in 1885. It has been enlarged several times since, now covering 6641 sq. km., and has been declared a World Heritage Site by UNESCO.

There are many ways to camp: camper, tent, bivy, igloo, or quinzee. How to build a quinzee: pile up snow to about 1.5 m; let it settle and freeze for an hour; dig out an interior chamber to desired size. It will be warmer and quieter than a tent, and faster and easier to build than an igloo. Upper Kananaskis Lake.

Is winter camping great fun? Even Polar Bears hibernate to avoid winter's chill! But Polar Bears do not have sleeping bags good to –25°C, foamies and tents, like we do. It is a challenge that, especially, young people take gladly, to prove that "I can do it!" The Valley of the Ten Peaks" – Banff National Park.

Above: Barrier Lake, in the northern part of Kananaskis Country, is a man-made reservoir to generate electricity. It is, as well, a great recreational area – especially for water sports: boating, canoeing and fishing, as well as hiking, climbing and cross-country skiing.

Left: Awesome and flamboyant, lofty Mt. Christie (3103m), south of the Athabasca River and the Icefields Parkway, presents its snowy northeast face on a cold winter morning. Climbing this remote mountain is made easier thanks to a handy Fryatt Hut. Mt. Fryatt, Brussels Peak, Belanger and Lapensee are the area's other interesting climbs. Jasper National Park.

Banff, Alberta - a hub of Canadian skiing, and other winter and summer sports, and tourist activities. Photographed on a winter night from Mt. Norquay. Good old Mt. Rundle (2998m) catches the last rays of alpine glow, long after sunset.

Another marvel of the Rockies, Lake Louise, and its famous Chateau. Snowy Mt. Richardson (3086m) watches this busy place in early winter. In a few days, the lake will freeze, letting skiers and skaters have some fun. Banff National Park.

Above: Anybody driving the Icefields Parkway to Jasper ought to stop for the "must see" mesmerizing Peyto Lake. It's a place like no other – the viewpoint overlooking the lake is high up, providing almost a bird's-eye view. To the left stands Caldron Peak (2917m); on the right is Mt. Patterson (3197m).

Left: Bow Lake is a large body of water at a high elevation, where winds are strong and common. That is a prologue to an explanation of how difficult it is to get a perfect reflection here. This photo is nearly good – the lack of a perfect reflection is compensated for by interesting light, colour and mood. In the background stands Crowfoot Mtn. (3050m).

Above: A mysterious dusk at First Vermilion Lake. Three Vermilion Lakes being at the doorstep of Banff, display an amazing variety of wildlife. You will see the most at dawn, or dusk. The small island is a calving ground for Elk. Bald Eagles and Ospreys nest, Beaver and Muskrat dwell, and Deer frequent the area, and Waterfowl are plentiful. Coyotes, Wolves and Bears hunt food here.

Left: A large cataract on the Athabasca River – the Athabasca Falls, in the central part of Jasper National Park, is a well-known tourist attraction. Several different viewpoints allow the falls to be seen from different angles. The massive falls, on the large river, causes vapour and mist to fall on the canyon's rock, making it very slippery. That is how accidents happen here – caution is advised.

Above: The Aurora Borealis, or Northern Lights, a luminous meteoric phenomenon of electrical origin, can be seen in polar regions both north and south (Aurora Australis). The far northern latitudes, north of the 60th parallel, increase your chances of seeing the Aurora – especially during the long winter nights.

Left: Renowned for its beauty and charm, Lake Louise is known the world over. The northern part of this paradise features Mt. Whyte (2983m), Big Beehive, Mt. Niblock (2976m), Mt. St. Piran (2649m) and Little Beehive – all reflected in the unusually calm waters of the lake. Banff National Park.

Above: South of Lake Louise loom the steep walls of Fairview Mtn. (2744m). Little effort is needed to attain this mediocre summit from Lake Louise, via Saddleback and its southern slopes. The summit affords lovely vistas, clockwise: Haddo Peak (3070m), Mt. Aberdeen (3151m) and its glacier, Mt. Lefroy (3423) and Mt. Victoria (3464m). Banff National Park.

Left: Mt. Niblock (2976m) is a mediocre summit in any respect – not difficult to attain, but no walk-up, either. From Lake Louise, take the beaten path to Lake Agnes, follow the right shore to the end, and then enter the large scree slope leading to Whyte-Niblock Col. From there, the summit is attained by a short scramble to the right. Banff National Park.

More wonders of Yoho National Park – Lake O'Hara (centre), and Mary Lake (foreground), as seen from Mt. Schaffer (2692m), which stands southwest of the lakes. In the background are the steep slopes of Wiwaxy-Huber. This area is a treasure chest – wherever you go, something beautiful awaits you.

Mt. Bell (2910m) is a large mountain of modest difficulty, but it is too low to provide great vistas. Taylor Lake is not visible, and only the west end of Boom Lake is. The view here is to the northwest, towards Mt. Temple (3543m), 10 km. away as the crow flies. On the right is Panorama Ridge (2800m). In the centre, part of Lower Consolation Lake can be seen. Banff National Park.

Above: The Three Sisters is a three-peak mountain synonymous with Canmore, located just a short walk south from downtown. The Big Sister (2936m) presents a semi-difficult climb; the Middle Sister (2769m) is a pretty easy scramble; and the Little Sister (2694m) is a difficult climb.

Left: A nocturnal image of Mt. Temple (3543m), viewed from the north shore of the Bow River. Autumnal Golden Larches and a solid wall of healthy forest surround Little Temple, on the right. Mt. Temple is a big mountain, with a big view and is an even bigger experience when climbed. Banff National Park.

The Fairholme Range, with Mt. Peechee (2935m), east of Banff and south of Lake Minnewanka. On the left is the "beauty" of prescribed forest fire, on the lower slopes of Mt. Girouard. 25 years from now, these scars will be replaced by new, lush, green forest. Banff National Park.

Because of plentiful UV rays in the mountains, their sunrises and sunsets are seldom as colourful as over the Prairies. From Bow Summit (2069m), looking west toward pointy Mt. Chephren (3266m.), an unexpectedly colourful sunset takes place. If you return to page 10, you will see where a similar, unusually colourful sunset took place. Banff National Park.

Mt. Kidd (2958m) is a massive mountain consisting of north and south peaks, with many ridges, gullies and climbing routes. Only conquered in 1947, today, it is very popular with scramblers and serious climbers. Kananaskis Country is now a major centre for all sorts of recreational activities.

The southernmost Rocky Mountain National Park is Waterton – small in size but very big in beauty. A well-known landmark, The Prince of Wales Hotel takes centre stage. Mt. Richards (2377m) looms above, and the Bosporus Strait, dividing Upper and Middle Waterton Lakes, is on the left. Fauna here is plentiful as is sunny weather.

Above: Frightening and dangerous, but fascinating, lightning is the discharge of highly electrified clouds in the form of a large spark, or flash. Lightning targets the ground, or another cloud, and is often associated with heavy rain. These "fireworks" occurred over Mt. Temple, near Lake Louise. Banff National Park.

Left: Polaris, or the North Star, is another celestial phenomenon high on a photographer's list. Polaris moves only slightly, but all adjoining stars circle around it – the farther they are from Polaris, the larger the circle they draw. The horizon is decorated by the shy Northern Lights. Taken in December, by the 58th north parallel.

Above: From Jasper, take the Edith Cavell Road south – high up, by the youth hostel, begins a major trail west, toward Tonquin Valley and the Amethyst Lakes. While there, climb Mt. Clitheroe (2747m) and you will see the above scene. North Amethyst Lake (centre), Moat Lake (right) and the spectacular The Ramparts directly ahead. Jasper National Park.

Left: Bow Lake, by the Icefields Parkway, has so many fine views that an entire book on the subject could easily be justified. On the left is the western part of Crowfoot Mtn. (3050m), in the centre-left is Portal Peak (2790m), and on the right is Mt. Thompson (3065m). All three mountains are sentinels, guarding the great Wapta Icefield, which sprawls to the south. Banff National Park.

The Author

From an early age George has displayed certain artistic and musical talents, loved theatre, opera and poetry - but at the same time he gravitated towards nature and the mountains. This little creation presents all the above interests together. George always loved nature and its soothing magical powers, so he greatly enjoys serenity and peace in the midst of the Canadian Rockies. George is a mountain man; he hikes, scrambles, climbs, and explores mountain wilderness – always with camera at ready. He has climbed over 400 mountains, published 38 pictorial books and developed a lifelong strong special relationship with the mountains, so the rigors and hardship of mountaineering is enjoyable to him. He is a kind of masochist so pain is an integral part of his daily life. No pain, no gain!

Joining the Boy Scouts at the age of seven guided his life in the right direction and now his activities and publishing influences generations of young Canadians who follow in his footsteps. One can either go to a smoky noisy bar or to the quiet, inspiring and beautiful mountains.

George is an avid environmentalist who believes as Henry D. Thoreau did that, "In wilderness is the preservation of the world". He has planted over 3000 trees to make our increasingly gray world a shade greener and healthier. Would you follow his example? Plant a few trees on your property or sponsor tree planting programs. Have a wilderness in your backyard!

This book was created in Alberta by Albertans
Printed in China by Everbest Printing Co.
Text Editor: Sheldon Wiebe
Design: George Brybycin
Typeseting: K & H United Co.
First Edition: 2005
Copyright © 2005 by GB Publishing
All rights reserved
No parts of this book may be reproduced in any form
without written permission from the publisher,
except for brief passages quoted by a reviewer.
ISBN 0-919029-38-8
This is George Brybycin's 36th book.
GB PUBLISHING
Box 6292, Station D
Calgary, Alberta Canada T2P 2C9

Front Cover: Maligne Lake
Back Cover: Mt. Assiniboine
Page 2: Cascade Mountain